HAL•LEONARD
INSTRUMENTAL
PLAY-ALONG

AUDIO
ACCESS
INCLUDED

PLAYBACK+
Speed • Pitch • Balance • Loop

TRUMPET

Disney

Beauty AND THE Beast

To access audio visit:
www.halleonard.com/mylibrary

Enter Code
2369-6815-3986-5674

ISBN 978-1-4950-9613-6

Motion Picture Artwork, TM & Copyright
© 2017 Disney Enterprises, Inc.

Wonderland Music Company, Inc.
Walt Disney Music Company

DISTRIBUTED BY

HAL•LEONARD®
7777 W. BLUEMOUND RD. P.O. BOX 13819 MILWAUKEE, WI 53213

In Australia Contact:
Hal Leonard Australia Pty. Ltd.
4 Lentara Court
Cheltenham, Victoria, 3192 Australia
Email: ausadmin@halleonard.com.au

Visit Hal Leonard Online at
www.halleonard.com

ARIA

TRUMPET

Music by ALAN MENKEN
Lyrics by TIM RICE

BE OUR GUEST

TRUMPET

Music by ALAN MENKEN
Lyrics by HOWARD ASHMAN

BEAUTY AND THE BEAST

TRUMPET

Music by ALAN MENKEN
Lyrics by HOWARD ASHMAN

BELLE

TRUMPET

Music by ALAN MENKEN
Lyrics by HOWARD ASHMAN

DAYS IN THE SUN

TRUMPET

Music by ALAN MENKEN
Lyrics by TIM RICE

EVERMORE

TRUMPET

Music by ALAN MENKEN
Lyrics by TIM RICE

GASTON

TRUMPET

Music by ALAN MENKEN
Lyrics by HOWARD ASHMAN

HOW DOES A MOMENT LAST FOREVER

TRUMPET

Music by ALAN MENKEN
Lyrics by TIM RICE

THE MOB SONG

TRUMPET

Music by ALAN MENKEN
Lyrics by HOWARD ASHMAN

SOMETHING THERE

TRUMPET

Music by ALAN MENKEN
Lyrics by HOWARD ASHMAN